ALL AROUND THE WORLD
ALGERIA

by Kristine Spanier, MLIS

Ideas for Parents and Teachers

Pogo Books let children practice reading informational text while introducing them to nonfiction features such as headings, labels, sidebars, maps, and diagrams, as well as a table of contents, glossary, and index.

Carefully leveled text with a strong photo match offers early fluent readers the support they need to succeed.

Before Reading

- "Walk" through the book and point out the various nonfiction features. Ask the student what purpose each feature serves.
- Look at the glossary together. Read and discuss the words.

Read the Book

- Have the child read the book independently.
- Invite him or her to list questions that arise from reading.

After Reading

- Discuss the child's questions. Talk about how he or she might find answers to those questions.
- Prompt the child to think more. Ask: Much of Algeria is desert. Have you seen a desert? Would you like to?

Pogo Books are published by Jump!
5357 Penn Avenue South
Minneapolis, MN 55419
www.jumplibrary.com

Library of Congress Cataloging-in-Publication Data

Names: Spanier, Kristine, author.
Title: Algeria / Kristine Spanier.
Description: Minneapolis: Jump!, Inc., 2022.
Series: All around the world | Audience: Ages 7-10
Identifiers: LCCN 2020046999 (print)
LCCN 2020047000 (ebook)
ISBN 9781645279914 (hardcover)
ISBN 9781645279921 (paperback)
ISBN 9781645279938 (ebook)
Subjects: LCSH: Algeria—Juvenile literature.
Classification: LCC DT275 .S63 2022 (print)
LCC DT275 (ebook) | DDC 965—dc23
LC record available at https://lccn.loc.gov/2020046999
LC ebook record available at https://lccn.loc.gov/2020047000

Editor: Jenna Gleisner
Designer: Molly Ballanger

Photo Credits: Dmitry Pichugin/Shutterstock, cover, 8-9; mtcurado/iStock, 1; Pixfiction/Shutterstock, 3; Anton_Ivanov/Shutterstock, 4, 5; mehdi33300/Shutterstock, 6-7; Filip Fuxa/Shutterstock, 8; Volosina/Shutterstock, 10 (left); Nataly Studio/Shutterstock, 10 (right); faroukb16/Shutterstock, 11; Hemis/Alamy, 12-13; ambient_pix/Shutterstock, 14-15; Silver Wings SS/Shutterstock, 16; gulfimages/SuperStock, 17; Abdelmoumen Taoutaou/Dreamstime, 18-19; Thornton Cohen/Alamy, 20-21; Janusz Pienkowski/Shutterstock, 23.

Printed in the United States of America at Corporate Graphics in North Mankato, Minnesota.

TABLE OF CONTENTS

CHAPTER 1

DRY DESERT

Travel across a suspension bridge. Visit a home on a cliff. Welcome to Algeria!

suspension bridge

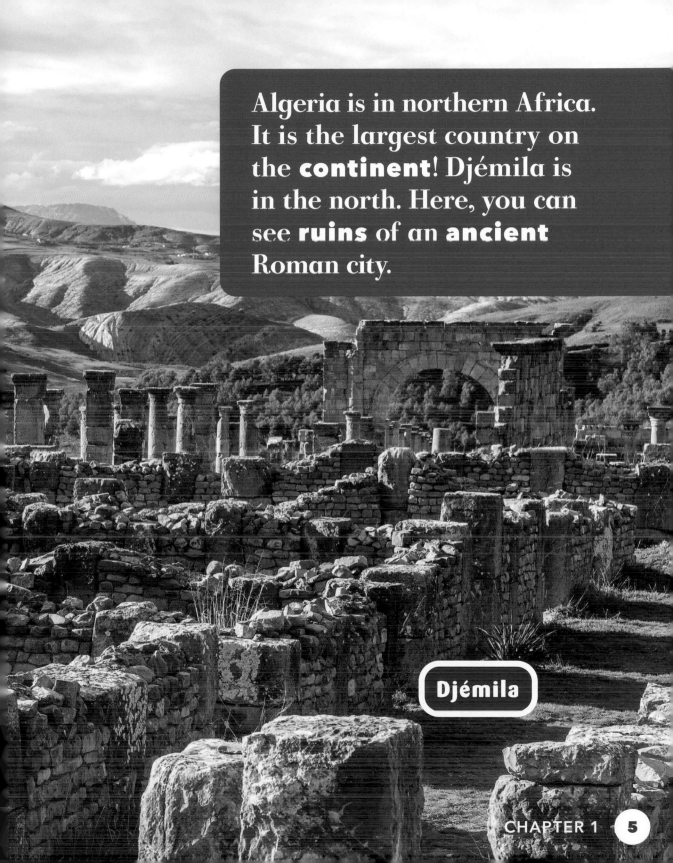

Algeria is in northern Africa. It is the largest country on the **continent**! Djémila is in the north. Here, you can see **ruins** of an **ancient** Roman city.

Djémila

Mediterranean
Sea

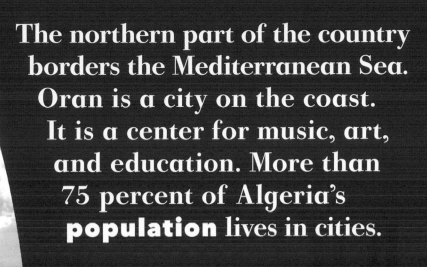

The northern part of the country borders the Mediterranean Sea. Oran is a city on the coast. It is a center for music, art, and education. More than 75 percent of Algeria's **population** lives in cities.

Oran

DID YOU KNOW?

People lived in the area we now call Algeria in 6,000 BCE. How do we know? They left behind cave art.

Look out for scorpions in the desert! The Sahara Desert covers most of the country. Hot, dry winds blow the sand. This creates large sand hills called dunes. They can get up to 2,000 feet (610 meters) tall!

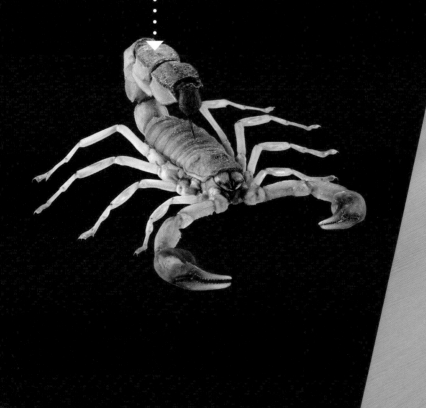

scorpion

CHAPTER 2
LIFE IN ALGERIA

It is difficult to grow **crops** here. Some people farm olives and dates. Others grow wheat, barley, and oats.

date

olive

People here eat borek. This is a meat pastry. Merguez is a sausage. Couscous is served often. People drink mint tea with their meals. Some enjoy Turkish coffee.

borek

Kids start school when they are six years old. Many have the same teacher for the first five grades. Most students go to school for nine years.

WHAT DO YOU THINK?

Many children in **rural** areas do not go for nine years. Why? They must help their parents with jobs or at home. Do you think this is fair? Why or why not?

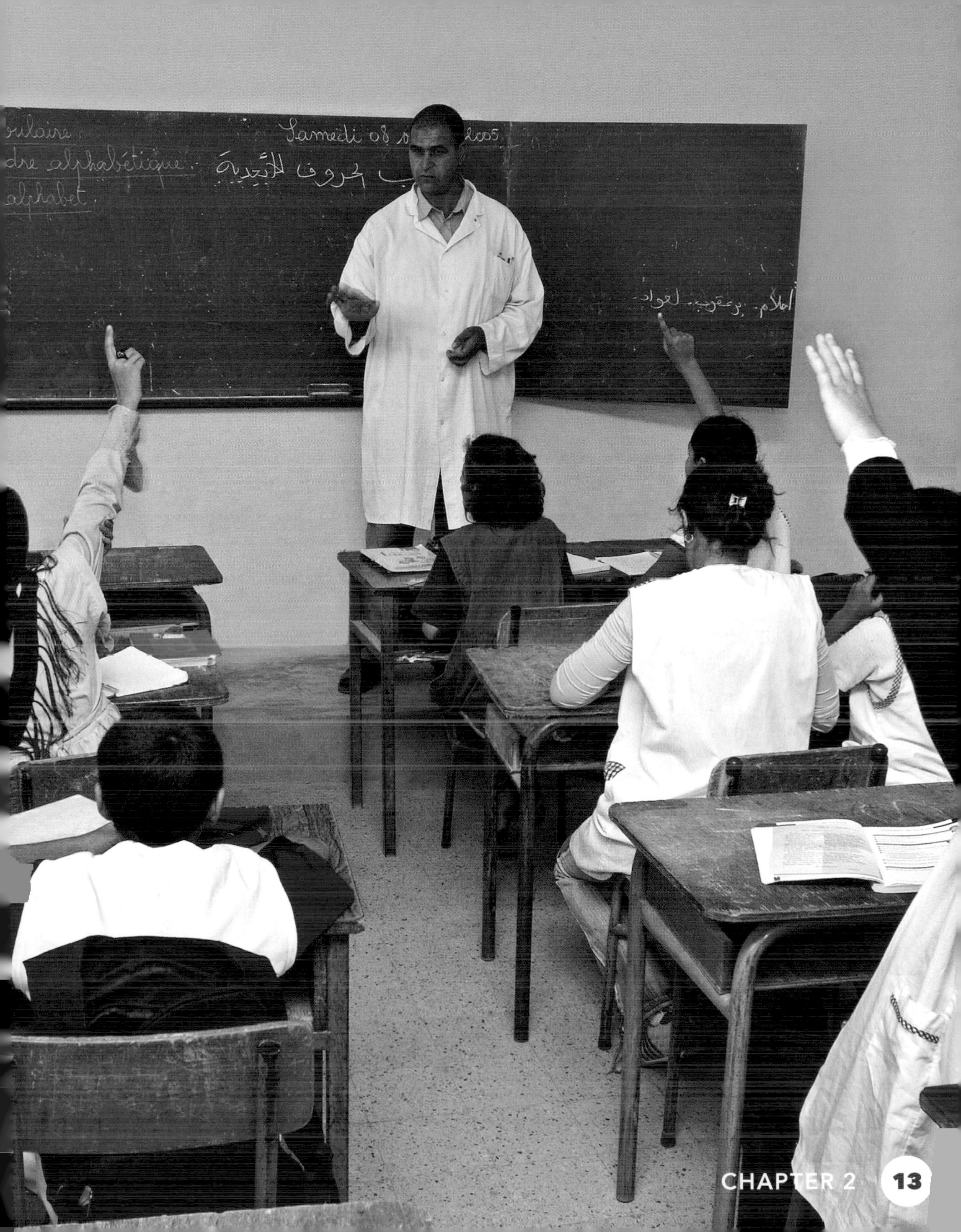

Algiers

Algiers is the **capital**. **Parliament** meets here. Its members make the country's laws. A president is the head of state. The president chooses a prime minister. How is this similar to or different from your country's government?

WHAT DO YOU THINK?

France took control of Algeria in 1830. A war started in 1954. The Algerian people fought for their freedom. They won in 1962. What wars has your country been in? Do you know why they were fought?

CHAPTER 3

FESTIVALS AND FUN

Most people here are **Muslim**. They celebrate Ramadan. It is a **holy** month.

During Ramadan, people do not eat between sunrise and sundown. In the evening, they visit with family and friends. They share a meal. Eid al-Fitr marks the end of Ramadan. This **festival** lasts three days.

July 5 is Independence Day. **Military** parades take place. People wear green. Why? This is the country's **national** color.

TAKE A LOOK!

What do the parts of Algeria's flag stand for? Take a look!

■ = Islam
□ = **purity** and peace
■ = freedom
☪ crescent and star = Islam, happiness

There is always time for fun! Many kids play soccer. Some jump rope and play hopscotch.

A popular style of music here is called raï. This is **traditional** folk music. It is played with drums and flutes. The songs are about living in hard times.

There is a lot to see in Algeria. Would you like to visit?

QUICK FACTS & TOOLS

AT A GLANCE

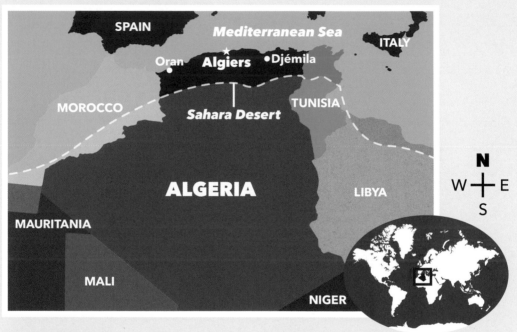

ALGERIA

Location: North Africa

Size: 919,595 square miles (2,381,740 square kilometers)

Population: 42,972,878 (July 2020 estimate)

Capital: Algiers

Type of Government: presidential republic

Languages: Arabic, French, Berber

Exports: natural gas, petroleum, petroleum products

Currency: Algerian dinar

GLOSSARY

ancient: Belonging to a period long ago.

capital: A city where government leaders meet.

continent: One of the seven large landmasses on Earth.

crops: Plants grown for food.

festival: A celebration or holiday.

holy: Related to or belonging to a god or higher being.

military: The armed forces of a country.

Muslim: People whose religion is Islam.

national: Of, having to do with, or shared by a whole nation.

parliament: A group of people elected to make laws.

population: The total number of people who live in a place.

purity: The quality of being pure.

ruins: The remains of something that has collapsed or been destroyed.

rural: Related to the country and country life.

traditional: Having to do with the customs, beliefs, or activities that are handed down from one generation to the next.

Algeria's currency

INDEX

TO LEARN MORE

Finding more information is as easy as 1, 2, 3.

1 Go to www.factsurfer.com

2 Enter "Algeria" into the search box.

3 Choose your book to see a list of websites.

FACT SURFER

ALL AROUND THE WORLD

Every country has an interesting history as well as unique places to visit. Learn more about how people live all around the world in these fun and fact-filled books. Have you read them all?

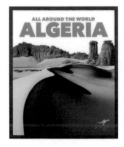
ALL AROUND THE WORLD
ALGERIA

ALL AROUND THE WORLD
AUSTRIA

ALL AROUND THE WORLD
BAHRAIN

ALL AROUND THE WORLD
FINLAND

ALL AROUND THE WORLD
HUNGARY

ALL AROUND THE WORLD
JAMAICA

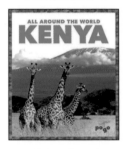
ALL AROUND THE WORLD
KENYA

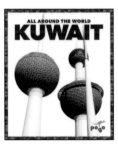
ALL AROUND THE WORLD
KUWAIT

ALL AROUND THE WORLD
LAOS

ALL AROUND THE WORLD
MADAGASCAR

ALL AROUND THE WORLD
NEW ZEALAND

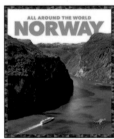
ALL AROUND THE WORLD
NORWAY

ALL AROUND THE WORLD
PANAMA

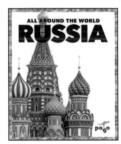
ALL AROUND THE WORLD
RUSSIA

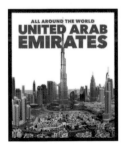
ALL AROUND THE WORLD
UNITED ARAB EMIRATES

ju^mp!

www.jumplibrary.com
www.jumplibrary.com/teachers

IL: Grades 2–5   ATOS: 2.7

ISBN 978-1-64527-992-1
90000
9 781645 279921